COOKBOOK
FOR DEPLORABLES

*Make the Kitchen
Great Again*

Scarlett Dunn

Ordering Information:
Quantity sales. Special discounts are available on quantity purchases by corporations, associations, and others. Orders by US trade bookstores and wholesalers. For details, contact the publisher at the address above.

Editing by The Pro Book Editor
Interior and Cover Design by IAPS.rocks
Illustrations by IAPS.rocks

ISBN: 978-1-7331796-4-5

     1. Main category—Southern Cooking, Comfort Food
     2. Other category—Political Humor

First Edition

SCARLETT DUNN BOOKS

TABLE OF CONTENTS

I'm Scarlett Dunn, and I approved these recipes.

Just for laughs!

BREAKFAST RECIPES

MAKE AMERICA GREAT AGAIN MUFFINS

INGREDIENTS

- 2 ¼ cups all-purpose flour
- 2 teaspoons baking soda
- ½ teaspoon salt
- 1/4 cup old-fashioned oats
- 1 tablespoon ground cinnamon
- ¼ teaspoon nutmeg
- 1 ¼ cups granulated sugar
- 1 cup vegetable oil
- 2 tablespoons melted
- 3 eggs
- 1/3 cup crushed pineapple
- 1 cup peeled apples, chopped
- 1 cup carrots, grated

- ½ cup coconut
- ½ cup raisins
- 1 ½ teaspoons vanilla
- ¾ cup chopped pecans

Set oven 375°F – Line 18 muffin cups with paper muffin liners.

In mixing bowl sift flour, baking soda, salt, oats, cinnamon, and nutmeg. In separate bowl add eggs, vanilla, butter, and oil. Mix well and slowly incorporate into flour mixture. Add sugar, carrots, apples, pineapple, coconut, raisins, and pecans.

Fill the paper liners and bake for 25 minutes, or until toothpick comes out clean.

HIGH ON THE HOG FOR ME BUT NOT FOR THEE BREAKFAST CASSEROLE

INGREDIENTS

- **20 ounces shredded, thawed hash browns**
- **1 pound cooked and crumbled sausage**
- **½ cup onion, finely chopped**
- **¼ cup red pepper**
- **8 eggs, lightly beaten**

- **1 (12-ounce) can evaporated milk**
- **2 cups cheddar cheese**
- **Salt/pepper to taste**
- **Add some red pepper flakes to kick it up a bit**

Brown sausage and in the last few minutes of cooking, add onion and red pepper. Cook for two or three minutes, then drain.

Layer hash browns in a lightly greased 9" x 12" dish. In a separate bowl mix together eggs, milk, 1 cup cheese, and salt/pepper.

Add the sausage mixture over the hash browns and pour the egg/milk mixture over the top. Sprinkle the remaining cheese over the top.

Bake at 350°F for 60 minutes.

PLANE LOAD OF DOUGH BISCUITS

INGREDIENTS

- **2 cups buttermilk**
- **2 1/2 cups all-purpose flour**
- **4 teaspoons baking powder**
- **3 teaspoons granulated sugar**
- **2 teaspoons salt**
- **1 stick of butter**

Preheat oven to 450°F.

Combine dry ingredients in a medium bowl. Add buttermilk to mix and stir until a moist dough is formed.

Melt butter in a 9" x 9" baking dish. Pour dough on top of melted butter. Spread evenly to sides with a spatula. Cut the unbaked dough into 9 squares.

Bake for 20 minutes or until golden brown.

SHIFTY SCHIFF SAUSAGE GRAVY

INGREDIENTS

- 1 pound sausage – I like a spicy sausage or an Italian sausage (use what you prefer)
- ⅓ cup flour
- 3 tablespoons butter
- 3 cups whole milk
- Salt/pepper to taste

Brown sausage in large skillet. After browned, add butter to sausage, stirring continuously. Add the flour to the skillet, mix thoroughly into the sausage over medium heat. Slowly add the milk as you continue to stir, bringing mixture to a boil, stirring constantly until it begins to thicken.

Lower the temperature add salt and pepper to taste. If you want to kick it up, add a dash of cayenne. Great over your Plane Load of Dough Biscuits. Not sure it'll taste like a billion bucks though!

CINNAMON DECEASED VOTER ROLLS

INGREDIENTS

Dough

- 1 cup milk, warmed
- ½ cup + 1 ½ tablespoons granulated sugar
- 1 tablespoon active dry yeast
- 2 large eggs (room temperature)
- 6 tablespoons melted butter
- 1 teaspoon vanilla
- 4 ½ cups all-purpose flour
- 1 teaspoon salt
- 1 ½ teaspoons cinnamon

Filling

- ¾ cup packed brown sugar
- ¼ cup granulated sugar
- 2 ¾ tablespoons cinnamon
- 6 tablespoons melted butter

Frosting

- 1 (8-ounce) package softened cream cheese
- ¼ cup softened butter
- 2 ½ cups powdered sugar
- ½ teaspoon vanilla
- Dash of salt

PREPARE THE DOUGH

Heat milk in microwave for 45 seconds. Pour milk into the bowl of your mixer, add 1 tablespoon sugar and 1 tablespoon yeast. Stir and let sit for 5 minutes until it looks foamy. Add ½ cup sugar to the bowl along with butter, eggs, and vanilla. Use a dough hook to stir until combined.

Add 4 cups flour to the bowl, along with salt and cinnamon. Stir on low speed, slowly increasing to higher setting. When a large ball is formed, the dough will be smooth and tacky to touch. If dough is too wet, add more flour, starting with 1 tablespoon, more if it's still too wet. Remove dough to a floured surface and knead for 5 minutes or until it's elastic and forms into a ball.

Grease a large bowl and place the dough inside. Cover with a warm towel and move to a warm place, allowing the dough to rise for 1 hour. It should double in size.

FILLING

In a small bowl mix brown sugar and cinnamon together. Melt butter in a separate bowl. Once the dough has doubled, roll it out on a floured surface. Make a rectangle about 12" x 24", about ¼" thick. Brush the melted butter over the dough, then spread the cinnamon / sugar mixture over that, spreading with a greased spatula. Roll the filled dough and cut into 2" pieces.

Line a 9" x 13" glass baking dish with greased parchment paper. Place the cut pieces in rows of 3. Cover again for 30 minutes; they will double in size again.

Preheat oven to 350°F. Bake approximately 20 minutes until golden brown. If top browns too quickly, lightly cover with foil.

CREAM CHEESE FROSTING

Mix cream cheese, butter, powdered sugar, vanilla, and salt. Hold at room temperature until rolls are removed from oven. Spread over rolls while they are warm.

KEEP YOUR DOCTOR APPLE BREAD

INGREDIENTS

- **3 cups all-purpose flour**
- **2 cups granulated sugar**
- **1 teaspoon baking soda**
- **½ teaspoon baking powder**
- **½ teaspoon nutmeg**
- **2 teaspoons cinnamon**
- **4 eggs**

- **1 cup oil**
- **1 teaspoon vanilla**
- **2 cups apples, chopped (I mix Honeycrisp, Fuji, and Granny Smith)**
- **½ cup pecans**

Blend room temperature eggs, sugar, vanilla, and oil together. Blend flour, sugar, baking soda, baking powder, nutmeg, and cinnamon together. Combine flour mixture and egg mixture together, then add pecans.

Pour into two greased 8.5" x 4.5" pans. Bake 55 minutes at 325°F.

CHUMPS CHERRY CHEESE DANISH

This is a great recipe for those mornings when you need something quick.

INGREDIENTS

- 1 (8-ounce) package softened cream cheese
- ¼ cup powdered sugar

Cherry Filling
- 2 cans cherry pie filling
- 2 teaspoons almond extract

Glaze
- 1 ½ cups powdered sugar
- 2 tablespoons milk

- 2 eggs (one egg used for wash on pastry)
- 1 package frozen puff pastry
- Almond slices

- 1 tablespoon cornstarch
- 1 ½ teaspoons lemon juice

- 1 ½ tablespoons lemon juice

Combine softened cream cheese with powdered sugar, add egg, and beat to combine. Roll out your puff pastry on floured surface until it measures approximately a 12" x 12" square. Cut the dough into 9 squares and place on a greased baking sheet. Add 1 ½ tablespoons cheese mixture to center of each square.

Mix cherry filling ingredients together and top the cheese with 1 ½ tablespoons of the cherry mixture.

Beat the remaining egg and brush the edges of each square. Bake at 350°F for 20 minutes, or until golden brown. While baking you can mix the glaze. Cool the pastry and add glaze. Top with almond slices.

It's those Chumps!

APPETIZERS

FAKE NEWS CHEESY FRIES

INGREDIENTS

- **32 ounces frozen French fries**
- **3 cups shredded cheddar and mozzarella cheese**
- **1 cup cooked and crumbled bacon**
- **¼ cup green onions, sliced**
- **Ranch dressing**

Cook French fries according to directions on package. Remove from oven and set oven to 400°F. Sprinkle cheeses over fries, bake until cheese is melted. Remove from oven and liberally sprinkle bacon and green onions over the fries when ready to serve.

RANCH DRESSING

- **½ cup buttermilk**
- **1 cup mayonnaise**
- **½ cup sour cream**
- **1 teaspoon garlic, minced**
- **1 teaspoon cayenne**
- **¾ teaspoon salt**

- ½ teaspoon pepper
- Dash of Worcestershire sauce
- *More heat – add a dash of hot sauce

Whisk together in a bowl and get ready to dip those yummy fries!

FREEDOM FRENCH ONION SOUP

<u>INGREDIENTS</u>

- **10 cups beef broth**
- **4 pounds yellow onions, chopped**
- **1 French baguette loaf, sliced into 1/2" slices (toasted)**
- **1 bay leaf**
- **1 ½ cups grated Gruyere or Swiss cheese**
- **1 stick unsalted butter, melted**
- **¼ cup all-purpose flour**
- **2 tablespoons extra virgin olive oil**
- **2 tablespoons balsamic vinegar**
- **1 ½ tablespoons Worcestershire sauce**
- **Salt and pepper to taste**

Place chopped onions in slow cooker and season generously with salt and pepper. Drizzle butter and olive oil. Cover and cook on high for 30 minutes, or until onions have started to caramelize.

In a small bowl, whisk flour into balsamic vinegar and Worcestershire sauce and mix until smooth. Uncover onions and pour in beef broth, flour mixture, and bay leaf. Stir everything together and cover. Reduce heat to low and cook for 6 hours. Taste for seasonings.

Ladle soup into oven proof bowls, top each with one slice of toasted bread, and cover with cheese. Place on top rack of oven and broil until cheese is melted and golden.

LEFT WING BUFFALO WINGS

A LOT OF HEAT, LITTLE MEAT

INGREDIENTS

- **24 chicken wings**
- **Oil for frying – vegetable or canola**
- **12 ounces hot pepper sauce**
- **1 stick cold unsalted butter**
- **1 tablespoon white vinegar**
- **2 teaspoons Worcestershire sauce**
- **½ teaspoon cayenne pepper**
- **Salt to taste**

Heat the oil in large skillet and add wings, cook about 6 or 7 minutes, turning once. Add remaining ingredients to pan and cook on medium heat.

Drain wings on paper towels, then place in a baking dish and coat with hot sauce. Bake at 325°F for 15 minutes. Serve with ranch or blue cheese dressing along with celery sticks.

*Want the sauce a little warmer (make them sweat)? – Add more of your favorite hot sauce.

START A COUP CABBAGE SOUP

INGREDIENTS

- **1 ½ heads cabbage chopped into ½" chunks**
- **14 ½ ounces fire roasted diced tomatoes**
- **4 carrots, chopped**
- **3 stalks celery, chopped**
- **1 small onion, chopped**
- **2 cloves minced garlic**
- **½ teaspoon red pepper flakes**
- **1 teaspoon salt**
- **½ teaspoon dried thyme**
- **½ teaspoon black pepper or to taste**
- **8 cups low sodium chicken or vegetable broth**

In a large pot add the olive oil over medium heat, then add in the onions and garlic and sauté about 5 minutes.

Add in the broth, salt, pepper, cabbage, carrots, celery, tomatoes, and pepper flakes. Simmer for 45 minutes.

ARROWS IN MY QUIVER LIVER PATE

INGREDIENTS

- ¼ cup mixture of olive oil and butter
- 1 pound chicken livers
- 1 small onion, minced
- 1 tablespoon celery, minced
- 2 hardboiled eggs
- Salt/pepper

Heat the oil mixture in skillet, add the onions and celery. Sauté until softened.

Add the chicken livers and cook, stirring until they are fully cooked and browned, about 6 minutes. Cool.

Add the liver mixture and cooked eggs to a food processor, pulse until coarsely chopped. Salt and pepper to taste. If the mixture is too dry, you can add a dash of chicken stock.

Serve on crackers or toast.

GRAFFITI GREEK SALAD

INGREDIENTS

- **5 Roma tomatoes, diced**
- **1 English cucumber, cubed**
- **½ red onion, thinly sliced and diced**
- **1 small yellow bell pepper, seeded, and chopped**
- **1 avocado, diced**

- **½ cup black olives, sliced**
- **½ cup Kalamata olives**
- **1 tablespoon capers**
- **Feta cheese, cubed**
- **1 cup garlic croutons**

Combine all ingredients and add Greek dressing.

GREEK DRESSING

- **½ cup extra virgin olive oil**
- **2 tablespoons red wine vinegar**

- **1 tablespoon fresh lemon juice**
- **1 teaspoon Dijon mustard**
- **1 ½ teaspoons minced garlic**

- 1 tablespoon minced parsley
- 1 teaspoon oregano
- 1 teaspoon honey
- Salt/pepper

Mix all ingredients in a jar or bender, pour over salad.

"PEACEFUL PROTEST"

BASKET OF DEPLORABLES DEVILED EGGS

ADD CAPERS AND CALL THEM RUSSIAN EGGS

INGREDIENTS

- **12 eggs**
- **¹/3 cup mayonnaise**
- **¼ cup Dijon mustard**
- **1 teaspoon apple cider vinegar**

- **Salt and pepper to taste**
- **Dash or two cayenne pepper**
- **Paprika**

Bring eggs to a boil, lower temperature to simmer for 12 minutes. Remove from heat and shock eggs in ice water, (makes them easier to peel). Once peeled, cut in half.

Mix all ingredients except paprika. Taste to see if you need a bit more cayenne. Stuff the halves and sprinkle with paprika.

Garnish with chives or bacon.

WHISTLEBLOWER WALDORF SALAD

<u>INGREDIENTS</u>

- **2 large crisp apples, cubed (I prefer Honeycrisp)**
- **½ cup grapes, sliced in half**
- **¼ cup golden raisins**
- **2 stalks celery, sliced into ½" pieces**
- **6 tablespoons mayonnaise**

- **¼ cup walnuts**
- **1 tablespoon honey**
- **Juice from ½ lemon**
- **Salt/pepper to taste**
- **Head of lettuce**

Mix all items together and fill leaves of lettuce (I use Bibb lettuce).

TRIGGERED MINI TACOS

TURN UP THE HEAT

INGREDIENTS

- **20 mini tortillas**
- **3 cups shredded rotisserie chicken**
- **½ cup cream cheese**
- **⅓ cup hot sauce**
- **½ teaspoon garlic powder**
- **1 teaspoon paprika**
- **Salt to taste**
- **Chives for garnish**
- **Mozzarella for garnish**
- **Sour cream**
- **Guacamole**

Mix shredded chicken, cream cheese, hot sauce, garlic powder, paprika, and salt. Fill tortillas and top with cheese, and bake at 350°F for 5 minutes.

Serve with sour cream, guacamole, or ranch dressing.

TERM LIMIT FRIED GREEN TOMATOES

INGREDIENTS

- **4 medium, firm green tomatoes, sliced ½" thick**
- **1 cup all-purpose flour**
- **1 teaspoon cayenne**
- **¾ cup buttermilk**
- **2 eggs**
- **½ cup cornmeal**
- **½ cup fine dry bread crumbs**
- **½ cup vegetable oil**
- **Salt/pepper to taste**

Slice tomatoes, salt and set aside for 10 minutes. Mix together buttermilk and eggs in one dish. In a second dish mix flour, salt, pepper, and cayenne. In a third dish mix cornmeal and bread crumbs together. Dip tomato slices into the four mixture, then dip in egg/milk mixture and dredge in cornmeal/breadcrumb mixture. In a large skillet add oil over medium heat, add tomatoes without crowding, and cook until golden brown on each side. Serve with a spicy ranch dip.

MAIN COURSES

TRUMP'S SUPERMAN SPAGHETTI WITH EXTRA BALLS

MAKE THEM *HUGE*

INGREDIENTS

Meat Sauce

- 2 tablespoons olive oil
- 1 onion, finely chopped
- 1 glove garlic, crushed
- 1 teaspoon mixed herbs
- ¼ teaspoon cayenne pepper
- 1 lb. ground beef / chuck
- 14 ounces Italian tomatoes, chopped
- 1 tablespoon tomato paste
- Dash of Worcestershire sauce
- 1 teaspoon dried oregano
- 1 ¾ cups of beef stock
- ¼ cup tomato ketchup
- ¼ cup red wine
- 2 tablespoons granulated sugar
- Salt/black pepper to taste
- 14 ounces spaghetti
- Freshly grated parmesan cheese

Heat oil and add onions, cook until softened, then add garlic, herbs, cayenne pepper. Add beef and brown. Once beef is browned, add tomatoes, ketchup, beef stock, red wine, oregano, sugar, salt, and pepper. Bring to a boil, then simmer for 30 minutes.

Meatballs

- 1 pound ground beef / chuck
- 1 pound sweet Italian sausage
- 2 eggs
- 2 tablespoons Italian parsley, chopped
- 1 tablespoon fresh basil, chopped

- ½ teaspoon red chili peppers
- 1 cup Italian bread crumbs
- ½ cup milk
- 3 tablespoons olive oil
- Salt/pepper to taste

Mix together ingredients and form into balls. Refrigerate for 30 minutes before browning in olive oil. Once balls are browned, add to meat sauce and cook covered for 30 minutes.

Serves 6

WHAT DIFFERENCE DOES IT MAKE NEW YORK STRIP STEAK

INGREDIENTS

- **New York strip steaks – good cut with some marbling**
- **4 or 5 tablespoons butter or vegetable oil (I prefer butter,** **but it will smoke at higher temps. You can mix the two)**
- **3 cloves garlic, finely chopped**
- **Salt/cracked pepper**

Preheat oven to 400°F. Allow your steaks to come to room temperature, about 20 minutes from the refrigerator. Salt and pepper both sides liberally.

Using a cast iron skillet, melt butter and sear steaks, 3 or 4 minutes each side. Add garlic to the skillet. Place skillet in oven, cook for 6 – 7 minutes for medium (145°F on meat thermometer). For medium-well, cook for 8 – 10 minutes. When you remove from oven, pour the pan drippings over the steak.

Let steak rest for 5 minutes before serving.

SAFE SPACE CHICKEN FRIED STEAK

INGREDIENTS

- **4 cube steaks**
- **1 ½ cups all-purpose flour**
- **1 teaspoon fresh ground black pepper, divided**
- **1 teaspoon salt**
- **½ teaspoon onion powder**

Steak Gravy
- **¼ cup oil**
- **¹/3 cup flour**
- **3 cups whole milk**
- **¼ cup heavy cream**

- **½ teaspoon garlic powder**
- **1 ½ cups buttermilk**
- **1 to 2 teaspoons cayenne**
- **2 eggs**
- **1 cup vegetable oil**
- **2 tablespoons butter**

- **Salt and pepper to taste**

- **1 teaspoon paprika**

- **Dash of cayenne**

Start with the meat by drying on paper towels. Salt and pepper the patties.

In one dish mix the milk with the eggs. In another dish mix the flour with cayenne, onion powder, and garlic powder.

Dredge the cube steaks in the flour mixture, dip in buttermilk mixture, then dredge back into the flour. Allow coated steaks to rest for a few minutes before cooking.

Heat oil and butter in a large skillet over medium heat. When it sizzles, it's ready to add the meat, a few pieces at a time. Do not crowd. Cook about 3 minutes each side to a golden brown.

Drain steaks on paper towels. You can keep steaks warm in oven set at 200°F while preparing gravy.

Chicken Fried Steak Gravy

Pour the grease from your skillet into a bowl, but do not scrape the skillet. Add back ¼ cup of oil and whisk in flour until a nice golden-brown color. Slowly add in milk and cream, stirring constantly.

Simmer until the gravy is creamy; you will be stirring about 7 minutes. If too thick, add more milk. Season with salt, pepper, and paprika. Pour over steak and serve with mashed potatoes.

LOCK HER UP LASAGNA

SHE WON'T GET THIS MEAL IN JAIL

INGREDIENTS

- **2 pounds ground chuck**
- **2 pounds Italian sausage mild**
- **1 (16-ounce) tub ricotta cheese**
- **1 (16-ounce) tub cottage cheese**
- **4 gloves garlic, minced**
- **3 eggs**
- **9 sheets lasagna noodles**
- **Freshly grated parmesan cheese**
- **16 ounces mozzarella cheese**
- **¼ cup Italian parsley**
- **Marinara sauce (recipe below)**

Preheat oven to 350°F. In large skillet, brown meat and add garlic, salt, and pepper.

In a mixing bowl mix egg, ricotta, and cottage cheese together.

Using a deep 9" x 13" pan, spread a thin layer of sauce on bottom of the pan before you place the first layer of noodles (3 across). Spread cheese/egg mixture over noodles, then add a layer of meat, and ladle marinara on top of meat layer. Sprinkle parmesan cheese, mozzarella cheese, and add some chopped parsley. Repeat for the second layer. The top layer will be noodles covered with marinara, then sprinkle with parmesan, mozzarella, and parsley.

Bake covered for 50 minutes, but uncover for the last 20 minutes.

*I have made this with uncooked noodles and cooked noodles. Both turn out great.

Marinara Sauce

- **1 (28-ounce) can whole tomatoes (crush yourself)**
- **¼ cup extra virgin olive oil**
- **2 tablespoons butter**
- **8 garlic cloves, chopped**
- **2 teaspoons red pepper flakes, crushed**
- **1 teaspoon salt**
- **3 tablespoons basil, chopped**
- **¼ teaspoon dried oregano**
- **¼ cup onion, finely diced**

Sauté onion in olive oil/butter in large pan, add garlic and sauté for a few minutes. Add remaining ingredients and simmer 45 minutes.

EMAIL SCANDAL EGGPLANT

INGREDIENTS

- 3 medium eggplants
- 1 teaspoon salt
- 1 cup all-purpose flour
- 1 teaspoon salt
- ¼ teaspoon pepper
- 3 large eggs, beaten lightly
- 1 cup panko bread crumbs
- 1 cup Italian style bread crumbs
- 1 teaspoon garlic powder
- 2 cups marinara sauce
- 8 ounces fresh mozzarella
- ¼ cup fresh basil, chopped
- ½ cup freshly grated parmesan cheese
- Vegetable oil for frying
- Italian parsley

Slice eggplant into ¼" rounds and place on paper towels, sprinkle with salt, and let rest for 45 minutes to remove moisture.

Preheat oven to 350°F. Pour a light layer of marinara sauce in a 9" x 13" baking dish.

Use three separate dishes for dredging the eggplant slices: one dish for the flour, salt, and pepper. The second dish will be for the eggs, and the third will be for the panko and bread crumbs combined. Coat each eggplant slice, first with flour, then egg, then bread crumbs. Place into hot oil and brown on each side. Drain on paper towels.

Add the browned slices to the prepared baking dish in an even layer. Add 2 tablespoons marinara to each slice, then sprinkle with mozzarella and parmesan cheese. You can layer or have a second baking dish and do single layers. Bake uncovered for 35 minutes if layered. For single layer cook for 20 minutes. Sprinkle with parsley.

COLLUSION DELUSION CHICKEN CASSEROLE

INGREDIENTS

- **3 boneless, skinless chicken breasts**
- **1 medium head of broccoli florets**
- **1 cup cooked white rice**
- **1 cup chicken stock**
- **½ cup water**
- **1 can cream of mushroom soup**

- **3 ribs celery, chopped**
- **½ cup onion, chopped**
- **1 cup sour cream**
- **10 ounces sharp cheddar cheese**
- **1/3 cup mayonnaise**
- **1 teaspoon garlic powder**
- **Salt/pepper**
- **2 tablespoon butter**

Preheat oven to 350°F. Add 1 tablespoon butter to baking dish and add chicken, bake covered for 40 minutes. Let chicken cool and cut into small cubes.

In a small pan, add 1 tablespoon of butter and sauté the chopped onion and celery. In a large mixing bowl, combine all ingredients, reserving 1 cup of cheese to sprinkle over top.

Spread mixture in a greased 9" x 13" dish, add cheese, and bake 35 minutes.

THE REAL COLLUSION

ERASE HISTORY HAMBURGER

<u>INGREDIENTS</u>

- **2 pounds ground chuck**
- **½ cup crushed panko bread crumbs or two slices white bread (crust removed)**
- **1 large egg**
- **2 tablespoons Worcestershire sauce**
- **3 tablespoons milk**
- **2 tablespoons ketchup**

- **1 ½ teaspoons salt**
- **1 teaspoon garlic, finely chopped**
- **½ teaspoon pepper**
- **1 yellow onion, sliced**
- **2 tablespoons olive oil**
- **½ teaspoon cayenne**
- **6 buns**

In a skillet over medium heat, warm the olive oil, add sliced onions, and cook until softened. Remove your onions and add chopped garlic. Cook for a few minutes.

In a mixing bowl, add bread crumbs or bread slices in milk until dissolved in a ball. Add egg, ketchup, Worchester sauce, garlic, salt, and pepper.

Combine the ground chuck and form into six equally sized balls. Flatten the balls into the size you prefer, then take the bottom of a spoon and make an indentation in the center. Cook about 4 minutes each side, until preferred doneness. The last few minutes of cooking, add the cheese of your choice.

Grill the buns and top with grilled onions.

HOT AIR HOT BROWN

INGREDIENTS

- 2 pounds cooked turkey breast, sliced thick
- 8 slices Texas toast
- 8 slices crisp bacon (pepper bacon is great with this dish)
- 3 tablespoons all-purpose flour
- 3 tablespoons butter

- 3 cups heavy cream
- ½ cup Romano cheese
- 3 tomatoes, sliced
- Salt and pepper to taste
- ½ teaspoon cayenne pepper
- Dash paprika
- Parsley, chopped

In a saucepan, melt the butter and slowly whisk in the flour until combined to form a thick paste. Cook the roux for 2 minutes over low/medium heat, stirring constantly. Whisk in the heavy cream and cook over medium heat, 3 minutes to simmer.

Remove pan from heat and whisk in the Romano cheese until dissolved. Add cayenne, salt, and pepper to taste.

For each oven proof dish, add two pieces of toast. Cover toast with turkey. Add tomato slices to the dishes and pour cheese sauce over the entire dish. Sprinkle the paprika on top and place under the broiler until browned and bubbly. Remove and add bacon to each serving, along with more cheese and parsley on top. (I often replace tomatoes with peaches).

PACK THE COURT POT PIE

INGREDIENTS

- **3 cups cooked chicken breasts**
- **3 cups chicken stock**
- **1 stick unsalted butter, divided**
- **2 cups onion, chopped**
- **1 cup carrot, chopped**
- **1 cup celery, chopped**
- **1 cup potato, diced**
- **8 sage leaves, chopped**
- **5 sprigs thyme**
- **1 rosemary stem**
- **1 cup frozen peas**
- **3 cups cooked, chopped chicken breasts**
- **½ cup flour**
- **¼ cup heavy cream**
- **¼ teaspoon paprika**
- **Salt and pepper to taste**
- **2 pie crusts (prepared)**
- **1 egg, beaten**

Bake your chicken, covered, in a 350°F oven for 40 minutes. Cool and dice. Leave the oven on.

Melt 2 tablespoons butter over medium heat in a large pot, and add the onion, carrot, celery, potatoes, sage, thyme, rosemary, paprika, salt, and pepper. Stir frequently until vegetables are soft. Add diced chicken and peas to mixture, mix thoroughly. Add remaining butter to pot along with flour, stir thoroughly. Remove herbs from mixture, then add chicken stock and bring to a boil. Reduce heat and let it simmer until mixture is thickened. Stir in cream, let it bubble for a minute or two, and add more salt and pepper to taste.

Grease a 9" pie plate and add one pie crust. Spoon all of the mixture into the crust. Cover with the remaining pie crust, crimping the edges together. Slit the crust on top and brush with the beaten egg. Bake 1 hour, until crust is golden brown.

DEEP STATE DUMPLINGS AND CHICKEN

- **1 whole chicken, cut into 8 pieces**
- **4 large carrots, diced**
- **3 stalks celery, diced**

- **8 cups chicken broth**
- **Salt/pepper**
- **Large pinch of poultry seasoning**

Cook chicken in stock pot with half of broth and half water for 30 minutes. Remove and pull chicken from bones. Discard skin and retain broth. Add back to the pot along with remaining broth, carrots, celery, poultry seasoning, salt, and pepper.

Dumplings

- **1 ¾ cups flour**
- **¼ cup vegetable shortening**
- **2 tablespoons unsalted butter**

- **½ teaspoon baking flour**
- **¾ cup milk**
- **½ teaspoon salt**

Combine flour, baking powder, shortening, butter and salt. Work with a fork until mixed well. Add milk a little at a time and mix until combined and you have desired consistency.

Knead on a floured surface until dough is smooth. Flour surface again as you prepare to roll out the dough into ¼" thickness. You can cut dough into strips, or you can pull it apart and drop individual pieces into the pot with the chicken. To thicken the sauce, you can add 1 cup heavy cream and/or you can make a roux with ¼ cup melted butter to ¼ cup flour and add slowly to the stock pot.

RUSSIA HOAX REUBEN

NO FAUX INGREDIENTS

INGREDIENTS

- **Corned beef cooked and sliced**
- **Sauerkraut (drained well)**
- **Russian dressing or Thousand Island dressing**
- **Swiss cheese**
- **Rye bread**

Heat the beef, cheese, and sauerkraut in a separate skillet before you place it on the bread. (Prevents soggy sandwiches.) Butter one side of each slice of bread, then prepare the sandwiches and grill in a skillet or a panini press. You can add the dressing before or after grilling.

MEDIA SUPPRESSION MEATLOAF

INGREDIENTS

- 1 ½ pounds ground chuck
- 1 small onion, diced
- 2 teaspoons garlic, finely chopped
- ½ cup milk
- 2 eggs
- 1 ½ teaspoons salt
- ¼ teaspoon ground pepper
- ¼ teaspoon red pepper flakes

- ¾ teaspoon basil
- 1 teaspoon onion powder
- 1 teaspoon dry mustard
- ¾ teaspoon thyme
- ½ cup panko bread crumbs
- ½ cup finely ground bread crumbs
- 2 tablespoons olive oil

Topping

- 1 cup loosely packed brown sugar
- 1 cup ketchup

- 2 tablespoons Worcestershire sauce
- Dash of white vinegar

In a small skillet, heat olive oil and sauté onions and garlic. Mix all ingredients together for the meatloaf, including onions and garlic. Form into a loaf and place in a 9" x 9" pan.

Mix topping ingredients and pour ½ of mixture over top of meat mixture. Bake 1 hour at 350°F. Warm the other half of topping and reserve for serving.

IT'S FREE FRIED CHICKEN

WHO FED THAT CHICKEN??

INGREDIENTS

- 1 whole chicken, cut into 8 pieces
- 1 ½ teaspoons ground black pepper
- 2 cups all-purpose flour
- ½ cup cornstarch
- 2 teaspoons salt
- 1 tablespoon paprika
- 2 teaspoons garlic powder
- 2 teaspoons dried oregano
- 1 teaspoon cayenne pepper
- 2 cups buttermilk
- 1 large egg
- 4 cups vegetable oil (do not use olive oil)

Rinse and pat dry chicken, then season with 1 teaspoon salt and ½ black pepper. Place into a large dish and cover with buttermilk. Coat thoroughly and chill overnight.

In a bowl, sift together the flour, 1 teaspoon salt, ½ teaspoon black pepper, garlic powder, onion powder, cayenne pepper, and paprika. In another bowl whisk together the eggs and ½ cup buttermilk.

Remove your chicken from the buttermilk. Dredge each piece in flour, then in egg wash, and back in flour again. Arrange on a baking sheet. Let stand for 30 minutes.

Preheat oven to 200°F. You will need an oven safe baking rack on top of a baking sheet to hold your chicken after pieces are fried.

Using a cast iron skillet, fill with ⅓" of oil over medium heat. When oil reaches 350°F, carefully lower chicken pieces into it without crowding. Fry dark meat and white meat separately. Dark meat takes a few minutes longer to fry.

Maintain oil temperature around 350°F. Fry chicken in batches. Cook for 10 – 15 minutes per side or until juices run clear. Remove cooked pieces and place on rack in the oven to keep it warm until finished.

CORRUPT CONGRESSIONAL CHILI

NOT AS MANY BEANS AS MILLIONAIRES IN CONGRESS

INGREDIENTS

- **3 pounds ground chuck**
- **1 medium white onion**
- **2 ½ tablespoons chili powder**
- **2 tablespoons cumin**
- **2 tablespoons chili**
- **1 ½ teaspoons salt**
- **1 tablespoon chopped garlic**
- **½ teaspoon pepper**

- **2 teaspoons red pepper flakes**
- **1 (15-ounce) can petite diced tomatoes**
- **1 (15-ounce) can hot chili beans**
- **1 (15-ounce) can mild chili beans**
- **1 (8-ounce) can tomato sauce**

In a large skillet, brown ground chuck and onions over medium heat. After it's browned, mix in garlic, chili powder, cumin, salt, pepper, and red pepper flakes. I like my chili on the warm side, but you can use less red pepper flakes if you like it milder.

In a large pot, add tomato sauce, beans, diced tomatoes, and sugar. Add meat mixture to the pot. Simmer for 1 hour. Some people like spaghetti in their chili. If so, cook about 4 ounces of broken spaghetti and add it to the pot for the last 20 minutes of cooking.

*You can also use premade chili powder (like McCormack) if you prefer not to add your own spices.

CRYING CHUCK CORNBREAD

GREAT WITH CORRUPT CONGRESSIONAL CHILI

<u>INGREDIENTS</u>

- **1 cup cornmeal**
- **1 cup flour**
- **1 ½ teaspoon baking powder**
- **1 teaspoon baking soda**
- **1 teaspoon salt**

- **1 ⅓ cups buttermilk**
- **2 eggs**
- **¼ cup vegetable oil**
- **¼ cup melted butter**

Melt oil and butter in a 9" x 9" metal pan or 12" iron skillet in oven set at 400°F. Mix all ingredients and add melted oil/butter from pan. Return all ingredients to pan, salt top of batter and bake for 20 minutes,

Great with chili or soup.

SOCIALIST SHRIMP SCALLOP FETTUCCINI

<u>INGREDIENTS</u>

- **6 ounces uncooked fettuccine**
- **½ pound uncooked medium shrimp, peeled and deveined**
- **½ pound scallops**
- **2 tablespoons olive oil**
- **1 tablespoon butter**
- **½ cup grated parmesan cheese**
- **1 cup heavy whipping cream**

- **¼ cup white wine**
- **2 garlic cloves, minced**
- **½ cup chicken broth**
- **Salt and pepper to taste**
- **½ teaspoon cracked red pepper (optional)**
- **1 tomato, diced**
- **2 tablespoons fresh parsley, minced**

In a large skillet heat olive oil and butter over medium heat. Once the butter is melted, add shrimp and scallops. Cook about 4 minutes until shrimp are pink and scallops are opaque. Remove from heat and keep seafood warm.

In the same skillet, sauté garlic for 1 minute, stir in chicken broth and wine, bringing to a boil. Reduce heat and simmer 10 minutes before adding cream. Simmer until thickened to consistency you desire.

Cook fettuccine according to directions. Drain thoroughly and add to cream sauce. Add the shrimp, scallops, parmesan cheese, salt, and pepper to the sauce.

Once on plates, garnish with tomato and parsley.

SLEEPY JOE GUMBO

INGREDIENTS

- 5 tablespoons butter
- ¼ cup all-purpose flour
- 1 small yellow onion
- 1 medium green bell pepper, chopped
- 2 celery stalks, chopped
- 2 cloves garlic, minced

- 1 pound andouille sausage, sliced into 1/2" pieces
- 1 pound large, peeled shrimp
- 1 tablespoon Cajun seasoning
- 4 cups chicken broth
- 2 bay leaves
- 2 green onions

Slice the sausage into ¼" rounds and brown them in 1 tablespoon of butter in a skillet.

In another deep pan, add onions, peppers, and celery and stir until softened. Stir in garlic and sausage, season with Cajun seasoning, salt, and pepper. Stir in bay leaf, diced tomatoes, and chicken broth. Bring to a boil, then reduce heat to simmer for about 1 hour. Add shrimp and cook until pink. Taste for salt and pepper.

Serve over cooked white rice and add green onions for garnish.

"IST" MISH MASH

INGREDIENTS

What the heck! Empty the refrigerator, throw everything into a pot, and see what sticks that day.

DESSERTS

FIXED DEBATE CARROT CAKE

<u>INGREDIENTS</u>

- 1 ½ cups dark brown sugar
- ½ cup granulated sugar
- 4 eggs
- 1 cup vegetable oil
- 1 ½ cups all-purpose flour
- 2 teaspoons baking powder
- ½ teaspoon baking soda

- 1 ½ teaspoons ground cinnamon
- ½ teaspoon nutmeg
- ½ teaspoon salt
- 1 teaspoon vanilla extract
- 2 cups carrots, grated
- 1 cup pecans, chopped

<u>Cream Cheese Frosting</u>

- 16 ounces cream cheese, softened
- 4 ½ cups powdered sugar
- 1 tablespoon heavy cream

- 2 teaspoons vanilla extract
- Pinch salt
- ½ cup chopped pecans for topping

*This recipe will make a two or three-layer cake.

Grease the 9" round cake pans.

Combine eggs, sugars, vanilla, and oil together in a large mixing bowl.

In a separate bowl, mix flour, baking soda, baking powder, cinnamon, nutmeg, and salt together. Gently combine liquid and dry ingredients. Add carrots and pecans.

Bake three pans at 350°F for 20 minutes – test with toothpick.

Bake two pans at 350°F for 30 minutes – test with toothpick.

Allow to cool completely before frosting. If frosting seems too thin, add more powdered sugar. Top with chopped pecans.

NANCY'S BEAUTY SALON
ICE CREAM SOCIAL

I had this ice cream dessert when I was in Venezuela *BS* (before Socialism). Perfect for a hot, humid day!

<u>INGREDIENTS</u>

- **Desired scoops of coconut ice cream in a 16-ounce brandy snifter glass**
- **Top with a variety of fresh fruit: melons, grapes, watermelon, bananas, strawberries, or pineapples.**

DEMOCRAT DOUBLE STANDARD DEVIL'S CAKE

INGREDIENTS

- 1 ¾ cups all-purpose flour
- 2 cups granulated sugar
- 2 large eggs, room temperature
- 1 egg white, room temperature
- 1 cup buttermilk

- 1 ½ teaspoons vanilla
- 1 teaspoon baking powder
- 2 teaspoons baking soda
- 1 teaspoon salt
- ¾ cup unsweetened cocoa powder
- 1 cup hot coffee

Sift together flour, baking powder, baking soda, and salt in a bowl. In a separate bowl, mix hot coffee and cocoa powder until smooth.

With a mixer cream sugar, buttermilk, and oil on medium speed until fluffy. Lower speed and slowly add the eggs, then add vanilla and beat until well mixed. Add the coffee/cocoa mixture and blend together. Slowly add the flour mixture to batter.

Pour evenly into two greased and floured 9" x 2" baking pans. Bake at 350°F for 30 – 35 minutes, until inserted toothpick comes out clean.

White Cloud Frosting

- 1 ½ cups granulated sugar
- 3 egg whites
- ⅓ cup water

- 1 ½ teaspoons vanilla
- ½ teaspoon cream of tartar
- Dash of salt

Mix together and whip for 5 minutes or until peaks form. Spread over cooled cake.

HIDIN' BIDEN BANANA PUDDING

<u>INGREDIENTS</u>

- **3 to 4 bananas (ripe, but not overly ripe; you don't want it to be mushy)**
- **1 (12-ounce) can evaporated milk**
- **1 cup granulated sugar**
- **½ cup all-purpose flour**

<u>Meringue</u>
- **6 egg whites**
- **1 teaspoon vanilla extract**
- **½ teaspoon cream of tartar**

- **6 large egg yolks – set aside the egg whites in the refrigerator**
- **2 ¹/3 cups half and half**
- **2 tablespoons butter**
- **1 ½ tablespoons vanilla**
- **Box of vanilla wafers**

- **5 or 6 tablespoons granulated sugar**

Whisk together evaporated milk, sugar, flour, and salt. Warm mixture over medium/high heat.

Whisk the egg yolks and the half and half together in separate bowl. Slowly whisk together with the warmed mixture. Continue stirring over medium heat for 15 minutes until custard becomes thick. Once it is custard consistency, remove from heat and add the butter and vanilla.

If possible, use a clear glass baking dish (makes an attractive presentation when you can see the layers). Line the bottom of the dish with wafers and arrange them along the sides of the dish as well. Top the wafer layer at the bottom of the dish with banana slices. Cover the wafer/banana layer with custard. Repeat for another layer.

With an electric mixer, whip the reserved egg whites, vanilla, and cream of tartar. Slowly add the sugar. Mix for 5 minutes until you see stiff peaks. Spread meringue over the dish and brown in oven under broiler (middle rack). It browns quickly.

Chill.

VOTER FRAUD FRUITCAKE

INGREDIENTS

- 2 cups all-purpose flour
- 1 ½ cups granulated sugar
- 2 large eggs, lightly beaten
- 2 teaspoons vanilla
- 2 teaspoons baking soda

Topping

- ½ cup butter
- ½ cup brown sugar, packed
- 1 cup granulated sugar
- 1 cup evaporated milk

- ½ teaspoon salt
- 1 (16-ounce) can fruit cocktail with syrup – do not drain
- ¼ cup maraschino cherries, sliced in half

- 1 teaspoon vanilla
- 1 ½ cups shredded coconut
- ¾ cup pecans, chopped

Mix together all cake ingredients and grease a 9" x 13" baking dish. Pour mixture into dish and cook 40 – 45 minutes 350°F. Test with a toothpick.

Combine ingredients for topping in a pan over medium heat and bring to a boil. Boil for two or three minutes and pour over warm cake. Smooth evenly with wooden spatula.

LIBERAL LEMON MERINGUE PIE

INGREDIENTS

- **1 cup granulated sugar**
- **2 tablespoons all-purpose flour**
- **3 tablespoons cornstarch**
- **¼ teaspoon salt**
- **1 ½ cups water**

- **2 lemons, juiced and zested**
- **2 tablespoons butter**
- **4 egg yolks, beaten**
- **1 9" pie crust, baked – recipe below**

*If you are making your pie crust from scratch, start with that and pre-bake. You can use a pre-made crust.

Lemon Filling

In a medium saucepan over medium heat, whisk together sugar, flour, cornstarch, and salt. Stir in water, lemon juice, and lemon zest. Stir frequently until mixture comes to a boil.

In a small bowl, whisk egg yolks and slowly whisk in ½ cup of the warm mixture.

Slowly add the egg mixture to the pan. Bring to a boil, stirring continuously until thick. Remove from heat. Pour filling into baked pastry shell.

Meringue

- **4 egg whites**
- **4 tablespoons granulated sugar**
- **½ teaspoon cream of tartar**

Pie Crust

- **1 cup all-purpose flour**
- **½ teaspoon salt**
- **2 tablespoons cold lard**
- **6 tablespoons cold butter**
- **¼ cup ice water**

Using two forks or a pastry blender, combine all ingredients. Flour your working surface as well as your hands and fold dough until blended. Once blended, cut in half and make a ball with each half. Cover with plastic wrap and refrigerate for a few hours. Roll out the crust and pre-bake for 20 minutes before filling with lemon filling.

Add meringue and bake at 350°F for 10 minutes. You can place under the broiler for a minute if you want the meringue more golden.

IMPEACHMENT PEACH COBBLER

<u>INGREDIENTS</u>

- ½ cup butter
- 1 cup all-purpose flour
- 2 cups granulated sugar
- 1 tablespoon baking powder
- 1 cup milk
- ¼ teaspoon salt
- 4 cups fresh peaches, sliced
- 1 tablespoon lemon juice
- 1 teaspoon ground cinnamon

Preheat oven to 350°F. Melt butter in a 13" x 9" baking dish.

Combine flour, 1 cup sugar, baking powder, and sugar. Add milk and mix well. Pour over butter in the baking dish.

In a saucepan over medium heat, add peaches, 1 cup sugar, and lemon juice. Bring to a boil, stirring constantly. Pour over top of flour mixture and sprinkle with cinnamon.

Bake for 45 – 50 minutes.

COCKTAILS

YOU MIGHT NEED THESE STRONG

MUDSLINGER

- **2 ounces vodka**
- **2 ounces coffee liqueur**
- **2 ounces Irish cream liqueur**
- **2 tablespoons chocolate syrup**
- **4 cups crushed ice**

Mix together in a blender. Pour into glasses that have been prepared with chocolate syrup drizzled on the inside.

Top with whipped cream.

RAISE YOUR TAXES TANGO BREEZE

- **2 ounces gin**
- **1 ounce orange juice**
- **1 ounce sweet vermouth**
- **½ teaspoon triple sec liqueur**

Combine all ingredients in an ice-filled shaker, strain in glass, and garnish with an orange slice.

QUID PRO QUO

- **2 ounces of good Kentucky bourbon**
- **1 ½ ounces cherry liqueur**

- **Cherries**
- **Juice from ¼ lime**
- **Cola**

Pour ingredients over ice in an old-fashioned glass and add an ounce or two of cola.

FISA COURT FIZZLE

- **2 ounces vodka**
- **1 ounce pineapple juice**
- **½ ounce lemon juice**
- **1 ounce simple syrup (see below)**
- **Soda water**

<u>Simple Syrup</u>
- **Mix ½ cup granulated sugar with juice from 1 lemon.**

Pour all ingredients into a shaker filled with ice. Mix well and pour into a Collins glass. Top with soda water.

LET'S LOOT LEMON DROP MARTINI

- **2 ounces vodka**
- **¾ ounce triple sec liqueur**
- **Juice from ½ large lemon**
- **Simple syrup (see below)**
- **Ice**

Rim the glass in lemon juice and dip the rim in sugar.

Simple Syrup

Mix ½ cup granulated sugar with juice from 1 lemon.

Combine all ingredients in a shaker with ice. Shake for a minute before pouring into prepared martini glass. Garnish with lemon.

DRAIN THE SWAMP DAIQUIRIS

- **6 cups ice**
- **½ cup granulated sugar**
- **5 ounces frozen strawberries**
- **¼ cup lime juice**
- **¾ cup rum**
- **½ cup lemon lime beverage**

Mix all ingredients in a blender. Pour into a cocktail glass, and garnish with strawberry.

LEAKIN' COMEY CRUSH

- **2 ounces orange vodka**
- **1 ounce triple sec liqueur**
- **1 cup orange juice**
- **1 ounce Sprite**
- **2 cups ice**

Mix ingredients and pour over ice in an old-fashioned glass.

Garnish with an orange slice and a cherry.

ILLITERATE RUBE INFERNO

Serve this to the "self-professed" tolerant intellectuals and watch the flames escape their afterburners!

- **1/2 ounce ginger brandy**
- **1/2 ounce rum**
- **4 or 5 drops tabasco sauce**

Serve in a shot glass.

RUSSIA RUSSIA RUSSIA WHITE RUSSIAN BOMB

- **2 ounces vodka**
- **1 ounce Kahlua**

- **2 ounces heavy cream**

Add vodka and Kahlua over ice in an old-fashioned glass, then add cream.
Serve with maraschino cherries.

SUCK IT UP BUTTERCUP SCOTCH

- **2 ounces Scotch**
- **1 ounce butterscotch Schnapps**
- **1 ½ ounces amaretto liqueur**

Pour over ice in an old-fashioned glass and serve.

"COME ON MAN" MAI TAI

- 1 ounce light rum
- 1 ounce dark rum
- ¾ ounce lime juice

- ½ ounce amaretto
- Mint

Add ingredients over ice, shake until cold, and pour into an old-fashioned glass. Garnish with mint.

ABOUT THE AUTHOR

Scarlett Dunn is the acclaimed author of historical Western romances including the Langtry Sisters series and the McBride Brothers trilogy. Her books have received starred reviews in Publishers Weekly and Booklist. She has also written a cozy mystery series set in beautiful bourbon country.

Scarlett lives in Kentucky but is a lover of sand and surf. She enjoys traveling, taking long hikes, cooking, reading, symphonies, and plays. She makes it a priority to Love, Laugh, Live.

Visit her website: www.scarlettdunn.com
I love hearing from my readers, so please leave a review with
your favorite retailer and tell me what you think!

ACKNOWLEDGEMENTS

Finding someone who gels with you as a writer is not as easy as one imagines. I am so fortunate to have Debra L Hartmann, The Pro Book Editor of IAPS. rocks, working with me. Whatever I throw at her, like the Energizer Bunny, she hops on and speeds away. Not only does she have great ideas, it's so much fun to have someone who laughs with me! Thank you, Debra. You are a joy to work with, and I'm so thankful you *get* my sense of humor!

I've made a lot of bourbon balls, but I must confess I rarely drink alcohol. For the cocktails, I enlisted the help of a few friends who are more familiar with alcoholic beverages. One friend in particular paid for his education working as a bartender, and he mixes a great White Russian! He is also responsible for the Illiterate Rube Inferno. You know who you are, and I'm grateful for your help. I will keep all names anonymous, lest people think you are the reason alcohol sales have soared this year. I may prefer tea, but I am a great designated driver!

SCARLETT DUNN BOOKS

CPSIA information can be obtained
at www.ICGtesting.com
Printed in the USA
LVHW021449090121
676042LV00008B/477

9 781733 179645